NO ACUTE DISTRESS

CRAB ORCHARD SERIES in Poetry
Editor's Selection

NO ACUTE DISTRESS

POEMS BY Jennifer Richter

Crab Orchard Review &
Southern Illinois University Press
Carbondale

Southern Illinois University Press
www.siupress.com
Printed in the United States of America

19 18 17 16   4 3 2 1

The Crab Orchard Series in Poetry is a joint publishing venture of
Southern Illinois University Press and *Crab Orchard Review*. This
series has been made possible by the generous support of the Office
of the President of Southern Illinois University and the Office of the
Vice Chancellor for Academic Affairs and Provost at Southern Illinois
University Carbondale.

Editor of the Crab Orchard Series in Poetry: Jon Tribble

Cover illustration: Matthias Clamer / Getty Images

Library of Congress Cataloging-in-Publication Data
Richter, Jennifer, 1969–
[Poems. Selections]
No acute distress / Jennifer Richter.
    pages ; cm. — (Crab Orchard Series in Poetry)
Summary: "A collection of prose poems and lineated poems that
chronicle everyday frustrations, confusions, and joys connected mainly
with motherhood and illness"—Provided by publisher.
ISBN 978-0-8093-3482-7 (softcover)
ISBN 978-0-8093-3483-4 (ebook)
I. Title.
PS3618.I364A6 2016
811'.6—dc23   2015033579

Printed on recycled paper. ♻

The paper used in this publication meets the minimum requirements
of American National Standard for Information Sciences—Permanence
of Paper for Printed Library Materials, ANSI Z39.48-1992. ∞

For you, Keith

Grateful acknowledgment is made to the editors of these publications, in which the following poems first appeared:

Brain, Child: "Birds Hopped Around on the Heap to Resuscitate the Tree"

Connotation Press: An Online Artifact: "Diptych: Ho Chi Minh City," "Leaving Thien Hau Temple," and "My Boy, My Body: When I Type I Always Mix Them Up"

Crab Orchard Review: "All Right, Good Night"

The Pinch: "Imagine" and "My Daughter Brings Home Bones"

Poetry Northwest: "Pleasant, healthy-appearing adult white female in no acute distress"

Prairie Schooner: "I'm Used to Feeling Like I'm Moving Even When I'm Still," "Mom into Fox," and "No Joke"

Sonora Review: "After You're Sliced in Two" and "I Always Think at First I'm Right"

Subtropics: "Mom, watch—"

THRUSH Poetry Journal: "I Find Myself Shelved between Rich and Rilke"

ZYZZYVA: "Hardy Boys Mystery #4: The Missing Chums"

I'm tremendously grateful to Jon Tribble, whose belief in my work sounds like one long resonant Yes. Every day at my desk I'm thankful for Bruce Weigl, wise mentor and dear friend, whose words continue to challenge me: "Say it clearly and you make it beautiful, no matter what." David Keplinger's careful eye, fine-tuned ear, and huge heart discover the best in my lines; he and Colleen Morton Busch reveal the best in me. Thank you. I'm grateful to comrades Karen Holmberg and David Biespiel; to B.T. Shaw, sister poet; to Amy Burrows, Rachel Kirby, and Shannon Bedford, right here by my side.

I'm grateful to those who helped craft this gorgeous home for my poems. Thank you, Erin Kirk New and Staci R. Schoenfeld. Thank you, Barb Martin, Karl Kageff, Linda Buhman, Wayne Larsen, Lola Starck,

Amy Alsip, Amy Etcheson, Bridget Brown, Lynanne Page, Lizabeth Engelmeier, Lana Fritsch, and Alyssha Nelson at Southern Illinois University Press.

Thank you to my inspiring colleagues and students, and my beloved friends and family. To my wonderful parents. To my husband Keith Scribner, especially: your abiding love heals me. This life we get to live is "miraculous," as Mark Doty says, "because anything/could have happened, and this did." Finally, to our children Luke and Chloe, two absolute beauties: in your bright light I bloom.

FAMILY HISTORY

Pleasant, healthy-appearing adult white female in no acute distress

Fancy seeing you here! my surgeon exclaims; his nurses roll their eyes above their masks. He drags a stool over, checks my line, winks *Hi, Smiley.* My chart notes say "cooperative." *Come here often?* Three procedures, two years. One doctor. His findings are significant: put me under and I'll laugh at anything. *What's a girl like you doing in a place like this?* He's warming up. He's counting down. It only takes till 8—heavy velvet curtains rushing shut. House lights: down. His whisper from the wings: *We've* GOT *to stop meeting like this.* Did you hear the one about the woman whose illness made her confuse happiness and sadness? When her doctor said How are you? she grinned, Never better. Then she wailed, Never better.

Mom, watch—

Pink drifts line the street where my son crouches, scoops, and
comes up flowering. His friend bends, too, eyeing the size of Luke's
pile. In this morning's storm, our plum tree dropped every wet
petal and now the boys face each other, throw open their arms,
collapse in laughter when the petals they hurl go up, not out.
Tossing, stooping, tossing: children move vertically in the world.
They leap into each deep puddle; they bet who can reach the
highest branch. They climb our tree all the time. When Luke fell,
I ran to him across the grass: a mother's life is horizontal. I drove.
I paced the waiting room, folded his coat. At home I pulled the
covers to his chin; I wanted him to stay that way, but our natures
aren't the same: in a moment, he was up. Now I'm always watching
that tree. More baby jays this year. Since he was small, Luke's
pointed to the sky, loved anything that flies. One by one, each jay
will fall. Or jump. I've watched the mother watch. I've watched her
shuffle back and forth along her branch.

I'm Used to Feeling Like I'm Moving Even When I'm Still

In the ferry's dim-lit belly we sit in seats our lives
have recently assigned: father driver, mother passenger.

Behind us, soothed by the boat's loud drone, the baby
finally sleeps. Yellow fluorescents stripe the hood, the dash,

our laps. We squint to get a glimpse of what's ahead; sea
spray on the windshield settles into salt. A bit of home—

damp waft of rumpled sheets—drifts in. Then fades.
Lately my body's felt docked, as in: all aboard.

When he leans toward me, the boat's black ramp starts
grinding down. Mothers pull their children from the rails.

Diptych: Ho Chi Minh City

1.
Reproduction

Like relatives waiting for a parade, a dozen
Mona Lisas line the curb of Bui Vien Street.
American Gothics, too, the daughter's moon-

face waning above each squatting painter.
Shopkeepers trail us like children, shuffle us
toward water lilies, melted clocks, starry darks.

As if I were a masterpiece, last night you pulled
the sheets off me in one grand sweep. *Let's try*
you whispered; then again this morning *Let's*

and now inside me vibrates Van Gogh's sky:
its glowing yolks and rush of swirling sperm
above a town of tiny people we can't see.

2.
Once a Mother

When a toddler fussing in his mother's lap
howls red-faced above the fan and Saigon

traffic, the quiet woman wiping tables
reaches to the altar on the wall—framed

painting: young boy, red tie, rouged cheeks;
incense, gladiolus, jackfruit, rice, bananas—

picks one from the bunch, bows, offers it to
the cry she can't stifle with/within her breast.

Leaving Thien Hau Temple

To load the bird with trouble—watch it fly
away for good—I've paid a man for one
brown sparrow pecking at its basket-trap.
(Dozens in there: if they all flapped at once
it might lift off. Imagine that relief.)
Pink tissue-paper flags curl toward the sky.
I prayed for years but now I'm winging it.
The man's cupped hand is feathered, beaked, alive;
the other one won't work. On Nguyen Trai Street,
we make a desperate little trinity.
The squirming bird bursts out, takes one quick spin
above the tiled roof then loops right back
into the crowded cage. My pain smirks *See?*
(It's singing now.) *You're nothing without me.*

These Days It's Hard to Tell What's Part of the Act

My doctor's packed the place for years
because he's known for making huge things
sometimes disappear. His routine is predictable,
effortless. Pick a number, any number: he's pointing
to his framed pain scale. He pauses for effect.
The six sequenced faces are a kid—time-lapsed—
at a magic show gone wrong. Onstage in Vegas
once, the rare white tiger snapped. Inexplicable:
my numbers creeping up each week. My doctor
backs out quickly, as if dragged off in some beast's jaws.

My Daughter Brings Home Bones

and piles them on the driveway: femur, rib, jawbone with a few flat teeth attached, dozens of thin arced parts. This is for me—40 today. My birthday sent her to the woods and back. Chloe leans in on her knees, arranges the bones along a concrete seam that leads out to the street. In this next decade, she'll go: head off like today, take into her arms all she's curious about. Her line of bones makes an arrow; sun lights them like a sign. She'll go: undeniable as these bones, baffling as what animal they'd make. She's on all fours. The way I labored: some wild thing. She lays out arms and legs; the bones in line make a spine. My height. On the driveway lies my body—when it held her—inside out. The way she came: like bones. Gleaming, after living in my dark. Gleaming. So I can always find her.

Still Life: Youth Correctional Facility for Girls

The windows mirror them: unyielding, hardwired
for toughness. Each a different glimpse of the outside.

Diagonal light snags their busted-Slinky-stretched-
along-the-ten-foot-fence background; barbed shadows

loop the kid-proofed common room. Its caged clock
stuck at time for Group. All in orange, they're spilled

from the same basket. Some are cut, though the blade
stays beyond the frame. Predictably dark green, tall,

a guard's inanimate behind them. This scene teaches
middle ground: share the molded plastic sofa, don't

sprawl across it like cascading grapes. The handmade
sign BEND LIKE A WILLOW is a fallen, crinkled leaf. Still—

this is better than what they left, too much movement
just out of sight. The one sitting stiff as a pitcher feels

even now his fingers squeezing tight around her arm.
In the shady corner: a peach clinging to her leaves.

After You're Sliced in Two

he spins the half of you that grins, then spins your fidgeting feet.
He pets each gleaming box. For effect, he walks between. Ta da—
he's done it again, your doctor. Women scream for him in their
seats. You've been together years: bright lights, the strain of the
blade, the *thunk* of his cut. Part of the act is you jumping out fine
each time. He'll latch you back together and with a flourish lower
the sheet. He can do anything.

ADMISSION

**Patient identified the following triggers: alcohol, cigarette
smoke, bright lights, loud noises**

An intractable migraine walks into a bar.
"Back again!" the bartender booms,
serves up the usual cocktail. It'll need

another round—always needs another,
stronger. It's grinding to the beat now,
knocking a few off their feet. "Some

nerve." "What a pain!" The migraine's
not responding. It's a regular, known
to stick around and shut her down.

Inpatient

All the other nurses flipped the switch to get us up: fluorescents
flared like pain. 5:30 A.M. They buzzed our beds; the motor slowly
made me sit. I was by the door so I was always first: they pulled my
blankets off, pumped the cuff around my arm, checked my pulse
where I wasn't attached to a bag. *Hmm*: the most they'd say. They'd
swing the trays across our laps, then leave. We'd wait an hour like
that for a hallway voice to come and show its face. But this nurse
was a sub—I saw her only once. (You'd left by then. They stripped
your sheets; my vitals took a dive.) That morning while I slept,
she found my hand in the dark and got the numbers for my chart.
I dreamed I waved; we drove away on mattresses. She tucked my
hand back in. The little sconce that she turned on made a V of
amber glow. *Honey,* she said, and I woke up crying. Crying: I was
that happy.

I Find Myself Shelved between Rich and Rilke

Who, if I cried out, would hear me among the angels?

> (the skies are full of them
> *going and coming and often staying all night,*
> levitating
> *under an open window:*
> a galactic cloud)

Ah, whom can we ever turn to?

> (heart sweating through my body)

Who, if I cried out, would hear me?

> (a woman trying to
> *listen to the voice of the wind:*
> untranslatable language)

Not angels, not humans—

> (accurately transmitted
> *voices, voices*
> whispering at last)

perhaps the birds.

Disappearance

Because she's not done growing, wings
on Shayna's bird tattoo stretch long
and faded on her thigh like nothing
strong enough to fly. *Wrong time, wrong*

place: how she answers Where you from?
Lockup: two more years. Fifteen; one
daughter on the outside and some
days—Road Crew stint, hypnotic sun—

she sees her flying by, a glimpse
of window-glinted hair and cheek,
I swear! It's true: that fast, more hints
of woman in my daughter keep

on surfacing. To her, it feels
like treasure rising from the wreck.
I can't get past what's lost. This week,
New Guinea divers claimed a speck

deep in their sea was Earhart's plane.
Some solo, Shayna scoffed. *Surprise:*
she brought a man; she crashed. Insane.
One day it won't be me who guides

my girl whose legs ache every night,
who lays my hand across her chest:
unbalanced recently, one side
still flat. Adult or child—undressed,

she's half and half. I ride her swells
of breath; I palm what waits, submerged.
A boundary issue! Shayna yelled
That's a boundary issue! when her

youth caseworker dialed the mother's
number then insisted he speak
first. Most calls play out like others:
Hell no—ask her aunt or even

She's dead to me. They looked for months
before they called Amelia's search.
I'm patted down each visit. Once
in class, Shayna described the birth—

her daughter not hers though she might
still recognize her mouth, her cry.
Mine sleeps facedown, arms out: in flight.
She meant *good night* but said *goodbye.*

Demeter Has Never Liked Family Game Night

CHESS

The removed piece is said to be "taken" or "captured." Strategy Note: It is unwise to bring the queen out too early. The cluttered field makes her more vulnerable to entrapment.

CHUTES AND LADDERS

If the pawn lands on that spot, it must slide down. CHUTES LEAD DOWN ONLY.

CHECKERS

Kings can "jump" to capture a piece. A player wins by either capturing all of the other player's pieces or putting them into a position where they cannot move.

CLUE

Your opponents might block any and all doors and trap you in a Room.

GUESS WHO?

On your turn you may ask who the Mystery Person is.

TROUBLE

The game continues to see who comes in second.

THE GAME OF LIFE

(Just as in real life, you can't go back in time!)

SORRY!

The WINNER scores 100 points if no opponent's piece reached HOME.

Hardy Boys Mystery #4: The Missing Chums

My friend (her daughter's gone again)
stays up for days scanning her firstborn's
newly posted photos (bragging captions,
exclamation points) for faces, streets,
a wallpapered hall that she can place.
This worked once: she tracked her daughter
to Seattle (background waves, September
rain). *They're taught to smell for sweat,*
my son (fisting tears away) tells me—
but there was no one there alive to find.
Ten years ago. He was two; I kept him
on my hip all day (West Coast sunshine,
birdsong) and had him nap on me
(two chests pressed together, wet).
To him this is a story (350 rescue dogs),
tense as anything he's read. *Their tails hung
down—you could tell they were depressed.*
He's used to endings like "At last their search
was rewarded." *So they'd feel better,
firefighters at ground zero played hide-
and-seek with them.* My friend's phone sits
clammed-up (dead? no) next to her bed.
Times like this (thousands of goodbye
voicemails, my friend's daughter gone
from her or gone, hearts busted into rubble,
my son's small shoulders slumped),
doesn't every mother think, Why
didn't I just say yes to everything?
(Kids pack up, carry every no.)
Why no ("we don't need a dog") when
my son's hopes were (are) my own:
someone to name and hold close, someone
who each time I call will come home.

I Always Think at First I'm Right

Armando Galarraga came within one out of a perfect
game Wednesday night, deprived of the milestone on a
call the first base umpire says he got wrong.
                                —*USAToday.com*, 6/2/10

Detroit's on its feet and screaming
for their pitcher, LOVE YOU
signs below the scoreboard's
lineup of zeros, zeros
hollow-mouthed as holes,
the rabbit hole for years

I stumbled into, drugged,
pain so record-breaking
it was hard to believe,
my family crowded into
gilded frames I fell past,
screaming, you following

me to rock bottom,
waving TOUCH ME signs
but I was that little door,
locked. How much of me
I saved for you: zero,
one long streak

on the scoreboard, two outs,
top of the ninth, Detroit
screaming on its feet, the batter
running out his grounder,
the ump at first swinging
his arms out—safe—

I knew what was at stake.
I'm sorry. Unbelievable:
your mouth all this time, shut,
the crowd around you wild
behind their flimsy signs, LOVE
that's trashed when things go bad.

Relapse:
    Behind Bars

each   night
is a tunnel half-dug
possible
                collapse
at   any   time
you're
watched
too   quiet   too
fidgety   sleep too
much   but
they're   too easy
            to fool
tuck in   a dummy
body   hide
all physical evidence
            your family
in dreams   reaches
out   to help
so   you chip
your pain
            into pieces
hand   it   over
in bags that
tick   and   ticktick
            then blow
Let me   out
you wake mouthing
and I'll
quit
hurting   people

The Only Other Thing to Watch

for June

After trying for your vein five times, the night nurse calls in
backup. The specialist, smiling like a waitress, brings a PICC line
on a silver tray. You moan. We both knew this was coming. A PICC
line means long-term. It means, Unpack your toiletries, Fill out
another week of meal requests. She tilts it toward you like a platter
of desserts, then rests the edge on your bed. A thin white tube is
the one choice left. All eyes on you—like passing an accident. Tony
Soprano is the only other thing to watch; he shoves a begging man
into a chair. The PICC line means, We're headed for your heart.
Tony cocks an arm. The heart: fist-sized and beating. Our window
with its blinds: an eye shut tight. *No, please* our TV screams; it
dilates when I click it off. From here I see you in its black. Just like
that you're trapped.

EXAMINATION

Chief Complaint

How many doctors does it take to screw in a lightbulb?

None—what doctor has time for that?
They all have to work on their patients.

Eighteen Seconds

Patients, on average, have 18 seconds to talk to a doctor
before they are interrupted.

—*New York Times*, 11/30/05

1.
It started right here, the back of my head.
The ache, the throb, the stab: it isn't those
that keep me up. I'm in a separate bed.
(Fragile. Don't Touch. Perishable.) We make
our kids keep quiet inside. Nobody's fine.
You know that ad—some New York hospital—
a family's silhouette in sepia?
*Think how many hearts are saved by treating
only one.* How many more are wrecked
with every round of inconclusive tests?

2.
I guess there is some family history.
(My father in the waiting room looked down,
nodded. I filled depression's circle black.)
I'd say I'm happiest when heading here.
This is where I go in my free time. Now
I'm ready for Plan B. Happiness is:
something new to Google. Those who claim it's
a warm puppy also tell me that I'll
grow from this except my dad's still driving
me around and I still take a child's dose.

3.
I don't complain—don't want time off, don't need
more drugs. I've tried Depakote, Sinequan,
Zomig, Xanax, Toradol: fuck you. Fuck
your side effects, your scrips fanned out then dealt
to me for years. And Midrin, Flexeril,
Vicodin, Axert, Celebrex, Frova
that hooked me—what the fuck?—Fioricet,
Neurontin, Corgard, Effexor, and you
Skelaxin, Pamelor. Fuck Botox, too.
Ice works. Sometimes my neck gets too wound up.

4.

Strong gusts, rain—any force against my head
just kills me. (Weather never used to hurt.)
Five years this spring; how soon should I come back?
Would you say now I'm a good candidate
for radiofrequency—what was it?—
ablation? (As in: erosion? Damn wind.)
Five years? This spring? How soon will they come back—
those nerves—once they've been burned? What if they don't?
My body's dragging like a plastic sack
of batteries: they're dead or not, can't tell.

5.
You should see: my lawn this year's so healthy!
Mine's a healthy marriage. Me against my
body isn't healthy competition.
They have that healthy glow—people outside.
Hospitals turn healthy profits. My goals:
less healthy contempt for authority,
more healthy attitude and appetite.
(This pain results in plastic pitcher-mugs
with bendy straws and lids. One symptom of
I'm about to be discharged is no lunch.)

6.
(I keep one-upping my worst fear each time
I live through it. The latest: I know more
than you.) Last time we did C2–C3.
Since then it's like my neck's sunburned; I can't
wear scarves or collars but my head pain's down
to 4. I'd say that's worth repeating. Right?
(They tucked my hair into a cap. Facedown.
Then mask-talk: Raise your thumb if you feel this.
New Sharpie smell, a red dot marks the spot.)
It feels like that: singed, permanent. Bull's-eye.

7.

My therapist tried hypnotizing me.
Turns out I'm good at it. But nothing changed.
(Turns out with no results I tend to come
back anyway, though that behavior's not
rewarded.) Ten, nine, eight . . . how many weeks
until my next procedure? I'm no mind
reader. I've had to choose between two dooms:
accept the risk or call it good like this.
No more scenarios. I'm sick and tired.
At night we use white noise machines like hers.

8.

In most ways I'm like no one else. (Except
when I'm the caption for that overused
cartoon: I'm sorry, honey, not tonight.
The woman with an ice bag on her head,
a single squiggle on the husband's brow.)
I mostly dress up and undress for you.
Tell me: are you seeing other patients
just like me? On a regular basis?
What do we have in common? I'm desperate
to be a type: labeled, buttoned down. Nailed.

9.
You said no side effects but now I'm off
the drug and nothing fits; pants hang on me
as if I'm worse. (When I complained you said
compared to the population at large,
chronic pain patients have proven themselves
to be less active.) I don't recognize
what healthy looks like. I was gone for good
last night; my family in my dream had left
the house so I came back, did it myself:
stripped the hangers, bagged my clothes for strangers.

10.
I'm better since last time. I'm better since
I don't need naps as much. Even though I
don't need naps as much, I still have trouble
sleeping. Trouble sleeping is still better
than having trouble waking. Even though
I calm my kids and say I understand,
there's hardly anything I understand.
I understand their waking in the dark.
Their dark is sometimes and is always me.
I'm fine if you mean satisfactory.

COMPLICATIONS

Today's lack of response suggests that the patient is not a significant placebo responder

You've watched women—desperate
as you—take him in the bathroom,

open-mouthed, moaning, so sick
of being let down that they'll insist

with him they've never felt better.
Though he's a tease—all talk, no

action—every morning women
wake with his name on their lips.

You're waiting for The One. He's
out there, the ads of grins and picnics

promise. Now your TV announces
I've got good news and bad news.

The bad news is, he'll come with
baggage: warnings, increased risks,

possible sudden losses. And the
good news? (Live alone this long

and you talk back.) The good news is,
he'll definitely mess with your head.

Mom into Fox

Stroke: *n., v.*

She calls it only The Episode. The forest she roams could be
called a hostile environment: Before has been wiped out. Poof.
Magic. Just like that. Prowling the house at night is new, though
her complaints about dogs aren't. She travels solo now—offer her
your arm and she's all teeth. My kiss on her forehead is half an
inch from the leak underneath. *When will they quit asking me?* she
groans. *Who doesn't know the opposite of hot?* Curls up, tucks head
to chest, wraps around herself the fringed lap blanket. Bedtime
stories used to comfort me: anything can happen. Sometimes when
she talks she's gone. I can't follow. In the hospital I nodded, petted
her legs. Her hands have always been that small.

My Own Blood

> One of the first steps of surgery is to tape patients' eyes
> shut.
> —*The Atlantic*, January/February 2013

With me they skipped the tape; I woke too soon,
facedown, to someone else's blood (I thought
no body could leak like that and still be here

to see). They test my mother's vision: fine,
although she'd need my help to pick which coins
would make a dollar fifty-six. The cost:

it's possible that what she's lost is gone.
(When her blood leaked, it stayed inside
her head.) It's possible she's kept it all.

Our pain's the same, behind one eye. She knows
some studies trace mine back to her. Count 'em—
five times in post-op where she watched me sleep

like forty years ago, the name she chose
around my wrist. No one called us lucky
till we weren't—till after slim chance happened.

Her surgeon tries: *the opposite of bad
is?* I don't know this yet, but soon she will
come back to me and I'll get better, too:

both mysteries. *And can you tell me why
you're here?* He's flipping pages of her chart,
says *Get some rest* and leaves us in the dark.

Angles, Angels

Most days they'd descend together into tunnels
tucked below Chicago's loud grid—my father
and his mother below streets she didn't drive
but knew which stairs would lead them to her

bakery, post office, or the vast Marshall Field's
laid out like a Roman town: all thoroughfares
at right angles, predictable, though she'd always
keep him close. Today my father shops alone

and drives the roads someone like him designed.
He's a planner, like his mother with her lists—
his mind as measured as blueprints, so this surprise
MRI and its shady grays don't make any sense:

why his wife can't go home yet, why he's buying
food for just himself, why rooms loop the nurse's
station like a labyrinth. A child's why, why, why.
He traces the brain's dim tunnels, lost without her.

Bad Dream

after *Go home and try to get some rest*

  he drags upstairs the labeled plastic bag

jacketpursebookshoes nothing you need now

  his heart a slow *thuhThunk* against each step

he sinks into his bed though yours stays made

  I'm standing where I'd whisper you awake

tonight it's my calm voice *It's going to be*

  I don't want to be daughter without you

stand in your spot and nod at the doctors

  pocket your keys and knuckle your cold ring

heat up the soup Dad likes and tuck him in

  then sleep here while you're there oh Mom I'm scared

Birds Hopped Around on the Heap to Resuscitate the Tree

No one squints here in winter except
maybe today in the brighter gray.

Now the swing set's a stand of bones
balanced in our backyard. Now I can see

the yellow slide, the faded baby swing,
the lost kickball stuck in ivy at the fence.

Yesterday, one man aimed his chain saw
at our trunk; another man cut little slits

into our son's knee. We nodded to both,
then stepped back. Both took all day.

Our son had gotten used to hopping
to the couch. I'd gotten used to him—

thirteen—needing me again. Last night
we gave him a brass bell to ring for help.

The yard's a gnash of branches.
The light I expected but not the silence.

Symptoms May Include: Trouble Sleeping through the Night, Sudden Tears

Chest slick with cooling sweat you wake from dreams
of babies curled there in the sun, asleep,

but no. It's dark. You're in the hour of mouths,
this breathing house where years ago you'd wake,

breasts soaked, and rise to feed your children's cries.
You couldn't do that again if you tried.

What to Leave Out When You Call the Wildlife Rescue Line

Just like that, his crib-side voice is back:
high-pitched and hushed, your husband's
hovering over a trembling patch of tall grass

where you're not rolling kickballs anymore,
not filling plastic pools, not picnicking in tents.
Your kids are out; the lawn grows up too fast.

Easy for you to imagine the tiny possum's
letting-go: goodbye, baby-carrying body.
You're stranded on the same blind path.

You prowled years of wide-eyed nights,
crept routine loops between two mewling
mouths. Now you miss everything,

woke to find a newborn's dropped pink
sock on your back stoop. What's lost
is all you see. Help me find—he asks,

bursting in breathless—that one spill-proof
bowl you kept? He rattles cabinets, fussing
and flushed. Cries out to you for milk.

My Boy, My Body: When I Type I Always Mix Them Up

My son looks to the ceiling when they start his IV. It's funny, he
says, staring at a star nestled into a moon's crescent: why would
they paint it like that for kids when that couldn't ever happen? He
likes his surgeon's straight-talk as he's wheeled off down the hall.
All of us waiting are cuffed with children's names. The parents
who've been here before have packed snacks; they've chosen the
chairs that face the double doors. On the rack, a magazine asks
WHAT WOULD YOU HAVE DONE DIFFERENTLY? The surgeon finally
emerges with photos: the shadowed terrain inside my son like a
moonscape if the moon were smooth. He slides a pen from his
pocket. I fidget like I'm starved. With the tip he traces exactly
where my body, when I made Luke's, made it wrong.

RELEASE

Patient states she has some fear that she might leave without being helped

Whaddya call a woman who's quit wishing
but spends hours in a gown, her eyes on the door?

        (Lately when I don't know I say, *This is killing me.*)

You got me, says my doctor with a chuckle. *I give up.*

Imagine

The healer said to me: *it worked because you thought it would.* I
let him palm my belly and my chest; sometimes he shook and
closed his eyes. Inches above my skin, he'd sweep his hands like
smoothing sheets I couldn't see. I left our bed for years when I
was sick. I understood our children then: bed meant missing out;
bed felt like punishment. Now I sleep best at the edge—where
the healer sat to rest. Your hand reaches for my hip, holds on. Our
children's mouths sigh open in the dark. They're not surprised:
the healer touched me, and it worked. They've seen magicians—
beneath the sheet that's pulled away, something's always gone.

Synesthesia: The Way I See It

My twelve months sit around a tilted ring
that hovers, planetary, in the space
before me. Half a year away, May waits

the farthest and the highest from right here:
my ring's flat plane tips toward the month I'm in.
I make one counterclockwise loop per year.

The new one's numerals above that track
are starting gates. Lap 45 this May.
My numbers stumble on a crooked path:

my early 40s climb a ladder's rungs;
below, my 30s line a curvy slide.
My 20s: Escher's steps. Steep digits lead

past 10 to 15's solid landing, wide
enough to catch a breath and settle down.
We've orbited together 15 years.

A different starting gate, a different ring—
though our For Worse came first, I'm better now;
still trying to make sense of everything.

After that I love you will be a quest as well bye.

—computer-transcribed voicemail message

Scenes of where their journeys lead from here:
that got okayed. But not the tiny teardrops,
roman numerals and initials the warden finds
hidden in their mural's mountains, rainbow,

city street cracked open by a rose. On the wall
each morning, something new is painted over;
today another girl took one look then threw a fit
and quit. I called to say I'm late. Lockdown,

strip search—one of my brush's handles gone,
its soft tip shaken from the tarp. I'm counting all
I've botched: optimistic trysts starting *After that,*
each ending with *bye.* The girls know this routine,

flip their hair and shake it—naked—as if a lover
watches from the bed. Perspective is tough,
but their street leads believably to a pot of gold,
each coin sketched with a beloved's silhouette.

Demeter Accounts for This Year's Indian Summer

She'd gone; I'd answered with a killing frost.
Crops languished. Then she sweet-talked him to leave.
Fevered, she hurried home. Her steps melted
a clear path back. Even queens need mothers:
flushed as the sunset undersides of clouds,
she sank into my lap. Stayed there for days.
To think I often prayed for that: my kid
napping. To think I always watched her then.
One bite buried her.

Girls Overheard While Eating Gourmet Jelly Beans

Piña colada's to die for.
This one tastes like honey.
Honey soap. Ew, licorice—
my mom loves those. Some
Easter Bunny she is—every
year the same faded eggs
in our yard. At least yours
didn't make you go to church.
Pass that basket. Stick out
your tongue. Your breath's
like bubble bath. Ooh: try
passion fruit. They taste like
lip gloss but look like blood—
little beads of it. Creepy.
Ms. Willis said "ovum" twelve
times in Friday's class. I heard
she lives alone. This tastes like
—that's just sad—mango,
definitely mango. Alone with
all her weird tan human body
models, probably. Coconut!
Like some mini chicken came
and laid them. Don't try this
kind unless you have a taste
for apple candles. Licorice
doesn't get good, but it gets
better. My mom hangs on
now when she hugs as if I'm
going away for good. I wish.
Grape is like communion juice.
You know that boulder-rolled-
away story? If they put me—
aw, pink lemonade! All those
stands we had, all those boys

on bikes!—you know that if
they shut me in some cave
alone, I'd sure as hell find my
way out, too. Amen to that,
sister. Cookie dough oh my
god take me now. Whoa—
listen! Amen's got men in it.

Demeter Can't Stand *Where You At*

Surf brings out the girl in her—
mom mom mom
trying underwater handstands.

*Under. Far from. Like before except
beneath*: prepositions
tease me. *Together with. Without.*

Undertow: warning. No longer
mine mine mine
she's fickle and predictable as tides,

her just-left-him lips: sea blue.
Half of her is all I get
when I look up. Legs, wavering.

All Right, Good Night

for T. S.

> The last verbal message to the control tower—"All
> right, good night"—came after a crucial signaling
> system had stopped transmitting.
>   —Malaysia Airlines Flight 370 (*NYTimes.com*, 3/16/14)

All we know for sure is that you're gone.
We're looking up; we're searching. Once before

I saw a face—a stranger's—turn to sky:
ice storm, the black oak limb's death rattle. Crash.

Last words are rafts. Are facts. The hospice girl
leans in; your mouth won't close. The ear hangs on—

Tim, hear our pings. We check the monitor:
Departed Early. This is ground control,

we're standing by. Good night, mute moon. Hush, clocks.
And good night, box. Here below, may we find

peace. Let the sea and all that lies in it
resound. Let those who have a voice lift up:

We believe in unexpected sharp turns
at the end. Praise the certain, swift ascent.

No Joke

Saigon chickens cross the road to get to what's left of the rice.
From their perch in an abandoned shack they hustle, clucking, to
the neighbor bent before a small red altar at her door. She snips the
faded mums, dusts the photographs, mounds warm rice in bowls
then shares the rest. Ancestors sit grinning in their frames, the
path they walk with her not linear but looped: every moment holds
the other side. It's different, I know—her history of pain and mine,
the cloud of ghosts who share our homes, what we mean by being
saved. I know, too: we have our families to thank for where we
are. She sees me hesitate and laughs, shooing me to say *just keep
going, you'll be fine.* Health feels like stepping off this curb, wild
sea of motor scooters parting. I love it here. Chrome rushes by in
sparkling waves. At times I thought I might not make it back. Even
the quality of light is new, I've come so far.

Bruce Weigl's poem "The Impossible" and Mark Doty's "In the Form of Snow" are quoted in the acknowledgments.

Thanks to Bruce Weigl for leading me into "Leaving Thien Hau Temple."

The italicized lines in "I Find Myself Shelved between Rich and Rilke" come from the first of Rainer Maria Rilke's *Duino Elegies*, translated by Stephen Mitchell; alternate lines feature Adrienne Rich's poem "Planetarium."

In language and style, "Demeter Has Never Liked Family Game Night" copies each game's actual instructions.

"Imagine" is in memory of Vernon Bowlby.

"Girls Overheard While Eating Gourmet Jelly Beans" is inspired by Mary Szybist's poem "Girls Overheard While Assembling a Puzzle."

Other Books in the Crab Orchard Series in Poetry

Muse
Susan Aizenberg

Millennial Teeth
Dan Albergotti

Lizzie Borden in Love:
Poems in Women's Voices
Julianna Baggott

This Country of Mothers
Julianna Baggott

The Black Ocean
Brian Barker

The Sphere of Birds
Ciaran Berry

White Summer
Joelle Biele

Rookery
Traci Brimhall

USA-1000
Sass Brown

In Search of the Great Dead
Richard Cecil

Twenty First Century Blues
Richard Cecil

Circle
Victoria Chang

Errata
Lisa Fay Coutley

Salt Moon
Noel Crook

Consolation Miracle
Chad Davidson

From the Fire Hills
Chad Davidson

The Last Predicta
Chad Davidson

Furious Lullaby
Oliver de la Paz

Names above Houses
Oliver de la Paz

The Star-Spangled Banner
Denise Duhamel

Smith Blue
Camille T. Dungy

Seam
Tarfia Faizullah

Beautiful Trouble
Amy Fleury

Sympathetic Magic
Amy Fleury

Soluble Fish
Mary Jo Firth Gillett

Pelican Tracks
Elton Glaser

Winter Amnesties
Elton Glaser

Strange Land
Todd Hearon

Always Danger
David Hernandez

Heavenly Bodies
Cynthia Huntington

Zion
TJ Jarrett

Red Clay Suite
Honorée Fanonne Jeffers